TRIUMPH STAG

1970-1977

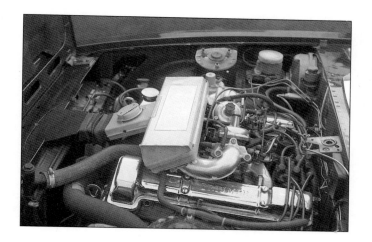

TRIUMPH STAG

1970-1977

◆

ESSENTIAL
ADVICE & DATA
FOR
BUYERS & ENTHUSIASTS

◆

James Taylor

Windrow & Greene Automotive

Published in Great Britain by
Windrow & Greene Ltd
5 Gerrard Street
London W1V 7LJ

A CIP catalogue record for this book is available from the British Library.

ISBN 1 872004 17 2

Design: *ghk* DESIGN, Chiswick, London

Printed in Singapore

Contents

INTRODUCTION AND ACKNOWLEDGEMENTS

Today's Stag owners are luckier than those who bought the cars when they were new. While it was in production, the Triumph Stag suffered from a number of maladies which its manufacturers were never able to cure. Since the car went out of production, however, specialists have developed solutions to all its problems. Running a Stag is now a joy rather than the nightmare it once was.

Several Stag owners made their cars available for the photographs in this book; a few others may be surprised to see a picture of their pride and joy! My thanks go to all of them, and of course, to the Stag Owners' Club who supplied yet more photographs. In particular, I am grateful to the people at the Heathrow Stag Centre: a friendlier and more helpful bunch of Stag enthusiasts you couldn't wish to meet.

The photographs on the front and back covers feature the Heathrow Stag Centre's painstakingly restored Triumph Stag and are used with their kind permission.

James Taylor
Woodcote, Reading, April 1992

The Author

James Taylor first began researching automotive history as a part-time activity in the late 1970s and has developed wide interests in both classic and modern cars. Now a full-time motoring journalist, he writes regularly for leading British motoring magazines and for several overseas publications. In addition to an earlier profile of the Triumph Stag, he has written books on Rover (including Range Rover and Land Rover), Riley, Citroen and Mercedes-Benz. Among other projects, he is currently researching and writing the first complete history of the Triumph Stag.

1.   Origins of the Triumph Stag

The Triumph marque was born in the early years of the twentieth century. Although the name was first applied only to motor cycles, the company soon turned its hand to the manufacture of light cars and, by the end of the 1920s, had made itself a reputation as a builder of cars which were just that little bit more sporting and elegant than the average.

During the 1930s, the company capitalised on this heritage, building a series of delightful sports cars and sporting saloons, but by the end of the decade it had lost its lead — not least to marques like the new SS Jaguar — and the company slid into receivership. After a brief spell in other hands, Triumph was bought by Standard in 1946 and was turned into the sporting arm of the Standard-Triumph concern.

Although the post-War Triumphs included some smart family saloons with a sporting bias, the company's greatest success was the TR range of two-seater sports cars. These sold extremely well in the USA, and on them rested almost the whole of the marque's post-War reputation. So charismatic was the name by the end of the 1950s that the Standard marque was dropped and all future cars from the firm were badged as Triumphs. It was into these circumstances, with the Triumph name riding the crest of a wave both at home and abroad, that the Triumph Stag was born.

The Stag story really begins in 1964. That was the year in which Italian stylist Giovanni Michelotti, who had produced a number of designs for Triumph since the late 1950s, asked the British manufacturer if he could have a car on which to base a Show special. There was nothing unusual about this — many other stylists built such one-offs which they then touted around the Motor Shows in the hope of attracting business — and the British manufacturer was happy to oblige.

The car Triumph found for him was a well-used example of the 2000 saloon, a 2-litre, six-cylinder, unitary-construction machine which bore a body styled by Michelotti himself. The actual car, registered 6105 KV, was probably a pre-production example dating from 1963, and its last duties for Triumph were in support of the works team at the 1964 Le Mans 24-hour race, from where it was driven straight to Michelotti's studios in Turin.

As there was no direct Triumph involvement in Michelotti's project, the factory expected to hear no more of 6105 KV. Then, over the summer of 1965, Triumph's Engineering Director Harry Webster went out to Turin on a routine visit and saw what Michelotti had produced.

As Webster recalled it some years later, what he saw in Turin was the wooden mock-up for the Show special. Part of the deal with Michelotti had been that Triumph would have first claim on the Show design if they liked it; and Webster liked it so much that he offered to buy it there and then. As a result, the finished car was prepared for Triumph and never graced a Michelotti Show stand.

As completed for Triumph, the Michelotti special sat on a shortened version of the original saloon's floorpan but retained its suspension and drive train. For the body, Michelotti had created a sleek two-door, four-seat convertible which he had set off with lilac pink paint and a set of chrome wire wheels. 6105 KV was driven back from Italy by

Giovanni Michelotti

The stylist who drew up the shape of the Triumph Stag had a formidable reputation in his native Italy before he first started working for Standard-Triumph.

Michelotti served his apprenticeship with Stabilimenti Farina in the 1940s, later setting up his own styling studio in Turin. He was a prolific and rapid stylist, and earned his reputation by drawing up complete body designs for the great Italian coachbuilders in the early 1950s. Bertone and Vignale, Allemano and Ghia-Aigle in Switzerland all made use of his services, and his name is associated with some of the most attractive bodies fitted to Ferraris in the first half of the decade.

Michelotti designs soon began to appear on cars built outside Italy. For Ghia-Aigle he styled the BMW 505 limousine, displayed at the 1955 Frankfurt Motor Show but never put into production. Later he worked directly with BMW on the rear-engined 700 models.

It was Michelotti who drew up the Vignale redesign of the Standard Vanguard Phase III, and Michelotti again who, in his own right, sketched up the Triumph Herald. Standard-Triumph's Harry Webster engaged him as the company's consultant stylist in the late 1950s (and an element of exclusivity was built into the contract). By the time he drew up the Stag, Michelotti had already produced several prototypes for Standard - Triumph and had drawn up the production Triumph 2000, 1300, TR4 and Spitfire. He would later go on to style the TR5 and Mark II 2000/2500, as well as several revisions to existing models.

(Photo of Michelotti: Giles Chapman Collection)

one of Triumph's senior engineers, Harry Colley, who claimed many years later to have been extremely impressed with both its design and its handling.

Harry Webster's next task was to convince his Triumph colleagues that the design had a future as a production model. They seem not to have taken much convincing, and were soon talking of selling as many as 12,000 examples a year if they could persuade American customers to take to the car. So it was that in the summer of 1966, the Triumph Board approved their Sales Division's formal proposal to adopt the Michelotti design as the basis of a production car.

Development work now began, and among the first refinements to the Michelotti design was the addition of a removable hard top which, Triumph hoped, would help the car to compete with the Mercedes SL models. After a brief period during which it was called a TR6, the new car was given its own code-name — Stag — which proved so apt for the image it projected that it was eventually carried through on to the production models.

Triumph eventually built nine more prototypes, of which the first was completed in 1967. But this and other early prototypes soon showed up serious body rigidity problems. Extensive use of double-skinning in the body structure presented a partial solution, but before long the Triumph engineers decided that the only really effective way to solve the problem would be to fit a bracing hoop between the door shut pillars. Even this did not completely eliminate the car's scuttle-shake, and further tests (initially conducted with a broom-handle!) showed that the best solution was to brace the hoop to the windscreen header rail. As a result, the production Stags all had this characteristic T-brace. Although it undoubtedly added to the occupant protection available in a roll-over accident, that was never its primary function, and the padded T-brace was always simply bolted to the tops of the B-pillars.

Although the Michelotti prototype was no slug-gard with its 2-litre engine, Webster wanted as much performance as he could get from the Stag. So the first Triumph-built prototype was equipped with the enlarged 2½-litre six-cylinder engine. This would give very respectable performance for the first production cars, and then, at some future

Above: Yes, it looks more like a car being scrapped than one being built, but this is the very first Stag prototype under construction in Michelotti's Turin studios.

Below: This three-quarter rear view of the prototype shows it at Canley in 1966, when it was being evaluated in the styling studio.

Below: After use in the development of the hard top and roll-over bar, the first prototype went back to Turin for conversion to a rather ungainly-looking fastback.

Above: Triumph built nine more Stag prototypes. This one is the second of them, completed in March 1968 and seen here wearing false number-plates. Note the twin exhausts, which were not carried over on to the production cars.

date, it could be supplemented or replaced by the new V8 engine which was under development.

The V8 was actually part of a new family of engines on which Triumph's Chief Engine Designer, Lewis Dawtrey, had been working since 1963. The aim was to save both tooling and development costs by developing an overhead-camshaft slant-four and a V8 which would in effect be two slant-fours on a common crankshaft. One or the other would be suitable for all Triumph's cars, for the capacities available in theory ranged from the 1½-litres of the smallest four-cylinder to 4 litres in the largest feasible V8. Although the V8 was far from ready for production, it made good sense to try it out in the Stag as early as possible, and so one of the prototype cars was fitted with a V8 engine — then being developed as a medium-capacity 2½-litre type — early in 1968.

Below: The roll-over bar was always simply bolted to the tops of the door pillars.

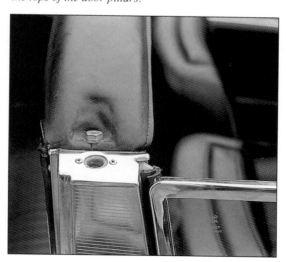

At this stage, Triumph suffered one of those changes of management which occurred with irritating frequency during the Leyland era. Harry Webster was instructed to take over as engineering chief of the Austin-Morris volume cars division, and Spen King — one of Rover's outstanding engineering talents — was drafted in to take over at Triumph. Seized of the need to sell the car in the USA, and well aware of the likely appeal of a V8 engine in that market, King pressed to get the V8 into production. Before long, the six-cylinder engines had completely faded from the picture.

As King recalled a few years ago, 'when I arrived at Triumph, they had the 2½-litre V8 in a car, and they were having trouble with the fuel injection system. The engine also didn't have enough low-speed torque. I suggested scrapping the fuel injection and going back to carburettors, and increasing the capacity to 3 litres. In the end, that's what we did.'

The extra power and torque from the bigger-bore V8 meant that other modifications were necessary, and both gearbox and back axle in the Stag had to be beefed-up to cope. In addition, bigger brakes were necessary and, to get adequate cooling, the Triumph engineers had to go for 14-inch wheels instead of the 13-inchers used on the 2000 saloon and the Michelotti prototype. All this added to the development time needed before the car would be ready for production.

Further time was consumed in experimenting with an alternative fastback bodyshell, and two different designs were tried in 1968-1969 before the project was shelved. After production had started, a third design was built up in prototype form; but the project went no further. It was probably cost and lack of development time which caused these plans to be scrapped.

Much of the Stag's detail specification was settled by the need to sell the car in quantity in the USA. As a grand tourer, it needed overdrive and automatic transmission options; power steering and electric windows were standardised, and one prototype was built with a power-operated hood, although that feature was not carried over into production. Wire wheels and leather upholstery were also agreed on as essential US-market options.

When the Stag project had first been taken on, the Triumph Board had envisaged production starting in 1968. But the constant specification changes had set the whole schedule back dramatically. The first production Stag, bearing commission number LD1 and later registered as RRW 97 H, was not built until November 1969; and the actual launch of the car on the European market did not take place until the following June.

2. Production history

Many cars have a chequered production history; not so the Triumph Stag, which remained fundamentally unchanged throughout the seven years of its production.

Many enthusiasts would argue that this was because its makers got the product right first time, and that argument has a certain amount of truth in it. The fact is, however, that the Stag was built during the British Leyland era, when Triumph was one of a collection of formerly proud marques lumped together into an organisation which appeared to do little but lose money. As British Leyland struggled to find its feet as a volume manufacturer, development money was poured into the Austin and Morris ranges, leaving none for the more exclusive ranges like Triumph's. The Stag, therefore, changed so little because there was no money available to spend on its development.

Yet there *were* changes to the Stag, and over the years it is possible to discern three major phases in the model's evolution. The first cars (which enthusiasts call Mark Is, although Triumph never did) were made between 1970 and February 1973. That month saw the introduction of the Mark II models, which were readily distinguishable by means of the differences listed below. Although cars remained Mark IIs as far as Triumph were concerned until production ended in June 1977, the 1976-1977 models were sufficiently different in detail for enthusiasts often to think of them as a third phase of the car's development. The reasons are set out below.

Mark I Stag

Minor changes were made to the specification of the Stag between its press launch in June 1970 and its market launch that autumn. Whereas the pre-production cars demonstrated to the press had 14-gallon fuel tanks, the production examples had a 12¾-gallon tank borrowed from the 2.5 PI estate car. The pre-production cars also had leaded-in seams between the rear wings and scuttle panel, while production examples had exposed seams. Both changes had probably been made simply to save on production costs.

The first cars were offered with convertible top, hard top, or both. Manual transmission was standard and usually came with the optional overdrive. Automatic transmission, also optional, actually proved more popular. Other options were leather upholstery and Delaney-Gallay air conditioning.

As introduced, the panels on the outboard edges of the Stag's seats were of smooth vinyl, but this was changed for a more luxurious-looking grained type after about 500 cars had been made. At the same time, stainless steel fillets fitted to the tops of the door shut-faces were deleted. Front suspension struts were modified early in 1971, and shortly after that the original single-point distributor was changed for a dual-point type. The water temperature warning light was discontinued in March 1971 because it was so inaccurate. (In fact, Triumph dealers were instructed by the factory to disconnect the warning light on earlier cars.) At the same time, new hood catches were fitted and the bonnet release was repositioned from the right-hand side to

Above: The Stag was designed to be a snug 2+2 Grand Tourer with its hard top on......or a smart open tourer with its top off. As the picture below shows, however, the side windows and T-bar gave plenty of protection from the elements to those sitting in the front seats.

Opposite page: The standard interior was plush, but functional. The combination of vinyl upholstery with wood veneer was typically Triumph.

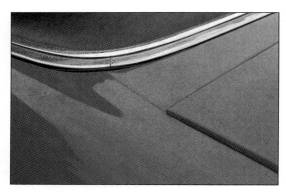

Above: If you find an early car which doesn't have these seams exposed at the rear, check it over carefully: it might be a prototype or pre-production example!

Above: Characteristic of the Mark I cars were these wheel trims, with black-painted panels. The actual disc wheels underneath had only four fixing bolts, in spite of the five dummy bolts on the trim! Note also the British Leyland symbol in the centre of the trim.

the left in anticipation of US-market requirements. With a new serial numbering system introduced in October 1971 came plastic glovebox hinges instead of metal ones, a revised central seat belt fixing and a new engine oil filler cap.

From January 1972, a bright stainless steel strip moulding was fitted to the body sills. There was a redesigned cooling system with a sealed radiator and expansion tank, and the system's pressure was increased from 13psi to 20psi. At the same time, the troublesome three-way by-pass hose was replaced by a U-shaped hose between the thermostat housing and water pump. The early air filter box with its twin 'trumpet' intakes was replaced by one with a single inlet incorporating a thermostatically controlled intake selector switch. Engine temperature operated this control, which moved a flap and allowed warm air to be drawn from the left-hand exhaust manifold or cold air to be drawn from above the radiator.

In October 1972, overdrive was standardised with manual transmission (although it remained optional in some export markets), and a Laycock J-type replaced the A-type fitted to earlier cars. This gave slightly taller overdrive gearing than before.

US-market Stags were introduced in September 1971. Their main distinguishing features were a lower-powered, emission-controlled engine and side marker lights in place of the front indicator repeaters and the rear wing 'Stag' badges. There were also plate-type badges below the rear wing marker lights, and alloy sill covers were fitted. The front seats incorporated fixed head restraints and knock-off chromed wire wheels were optional.

Left: Only cars made before January 1972 had this type of air filter box with its twin 'trumpet' intakes. The bright plating on this one is not an original feature.

Right: All cars made after January 1972 had a thermostatically-controlled air intake like the one seen here.

Above: A plain panel at the top of the backrest distinguishes Mark I front seats.

Right: Before March 1971, a water temperature light was included among the warning lights in the characteristically Triumph circular cluster.

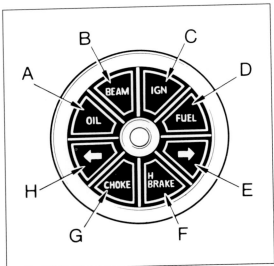

Left: The later warning light cluster had no water temperature segment.

Below: Mark I cars had courtesy lamps on the B-pillars.

Left: Number-plate lamps on Mark I cars were fitted in the plinth on the rear bumper. The car in this picture is actually one of the pre-production models.

Mark II Stag

The Mark II Stags appeared in February 1973. Most of the changes in them were cosmetic. The sills and tail panel were painted matt black, and twin coachlines (not painted, but stuck on) were added to the body sides. Black also replaced silver-grey as the background colour of the grille and rear wing 'Stag' badges. The standard wheel trims no longer had black-painted panels, and smart five-spoke alloy wheels became optional. In theory, wire wheels were also optional, but in practice they were very rarely specified on home-market cars.

From the rear, Mark II Stags could also be distinguished by their exhaust tail pipes, which had a smaller bore than the earlier type. The rear number-plate lamps had also been repositioned from the plinth on the bumper to the edge of the boot-lid and a smaller plinth, still bearing a Triumph badge, was fitted.

All cars now came with both hard and soft tops as standard. Sundym tinted glass was fitted all round, and the convertible top now came without its three-quarter windows (which had tended to split after becoming trapped during hood stowage). There was also a modified pantograph on the driver's side windscreen wiper.

Inside, the front seats had lost the plain panels at the top of their backrests and now incorporated fittings for adjustable head restraints. The upholstery material, while visually similar to the earlier type, was now flame-retardant, and there were ten panels in the basket-weave centre section instead of nine. A single interior light in the centre of the roll-over bar replaced the twin lamps on the door pillars of Mark I cars. All instruments now had chrome bezels instead of the matt black types on Mark I cars and the needles of the minor gauges pointed upwards instead of downwards. There was also a smaller-diameter steering wheel, intended to improve steering 'feel'. The 'parking lights' facility was deleted. The cigar lighter and carpets were changed, and Kangol seat belts were fitted as standard. The driver was given a left foot rest. Air conditioning and leather upholstery were optional.

The only noteworthy mechanical changes for Mark II Stags were a changed steering ratio, modified carburettors and a higher compression ratio,

Left: US-market cars had side marker lights and a different Stag badge on the rear wing. Some enthusiastic owners have also fitted them to home market models.

Left: Wire wheels were optional, but much more common on US-market Stags than at home. This car has been fitted with a non-standard bump strip along the body sides.

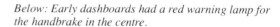

Below: Early dashboards had a red warning lamp for the handbrake in the centre.

Below: With the Mark II Stags came blacked-out sills and tail panel, as this contemporary publicity picture shows.

Left: Mark II Stags also had a twin coachline, with the upper line being thinner than the lower

Below: The standard wheel trims lost their black panels on Mark II Stags.

Left: Optional on Mark II models were these smart, five-spoke alloy wheels. This one was specially mounted and displayed by a proud owner at a Stag Owners' Club event.

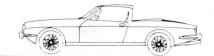
the last of which altered the engine's power and torque characteristics. To achieve this, Triumph had reshaped the combustion chambers and fitted dome-topped pistons.

US-market Mark II cars incorporated these changes, but had a lowered compression ratio to meet emissions-control regulations. The Stag was withdrawn from the US market in July 1973.

In January 1974, the hood material was changed to mohair with a fawn lining. A seat belt warning light and a hazard warning light system were added. Air conditioning was deleted from the options list in March 1975.

The "third phase" Stags were introduced in October 1975. There were new paint colours and alloy wheels were standardised. Wire wheels ceased to be available, and brushed aluminium cover plates were added to the body sills. The tail panel was now painted in body-colour once again, as it had been on Mark I cars. The handbrake lever grip was redesigned and the trip counter on the speedometer now had a push-button reset. Tufted carpet was now used.

From October 1976, automatic-transmission Stags had a Borg Warner type 65 gearbox instead of the earlier type 35. This change brought with it a new propshaft and modified front exhaust pipes, although the manual-transmission cars remained as before. All cars had a smaller radiator, anti-run-on valves for the carburettors and a changed steering ratio. Black inserts were fitted to the cutouts in the steering wheel spokes and stalk-type central seat belt fixings arrived. A new type of screenwash bottle was also fitted.

Left: There were plain rear quarters for the convertible tops of Mark II cars, although Mark Is had additional perspex windows. Many owners of early cars have converted to the later type because the additional windows are easily damaged.

Below, left: Mark II Stags had smaller-bore tailpipes than Mark Is. However, both large and small-bore types are now found on Stags of all ages.

Below: The number plate lamps were repositioned in the trailing edge of the bootlid on Mark IIs…

...and a smaller plinth was fitted to the bumper.

Mark II seats had basket-weave panels at the tops of their backrests and were designed to take adjustable head restraints.

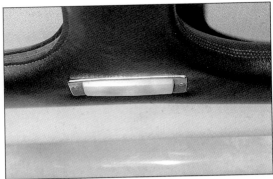

Left: There was only one courtesy light in Mark II cars, fitted in the centre of the roll-over bar.

Below: The post-January 1974 dashboard incorporated a hazard warning lamps switch and (on UK-market cars only) a seat-belt warning lamp in the centre. The handbrake warning light was now at the bottom right. Note also that the needles of the minor gauges point upwards; on Mk.I cars they hung downwards.

Left: Smart alloy sill covers were fitted for the last two seasons of Stag production.

The tail panel was in body-colour once again on 1976 and 1977-model Stags.

The very last cars had plastic inserts in the slots of the steering-wheel spokes.

3. Choosing your Stag

More than many other cars, the Triumph Stag suffers from rumour, myth and general misunderstanding of its weaknesses. The good news is that nowadays there is no weakness which cannot be rectified; the bad news is that there are still plenty of weaknesses to worry about. Before going to look at examples for sale, it is therefore advisable to read carefully through these guidance notes and, if you can't memorise them, take them with you!

Whatever else you do, it is vital that you resist the temptation to buy a Stag after a quick look-over. Owners have been known to tart cars up for sale, and there are plenty of hidden problem areas which you won't even think of examining unless you know about them. The best way to assess the condition of a car is by a systematic examination. (A check-list is provided further on in this chapter.) It does take time, but the seller shouldn't begrudge you that. If he does, you can bet that he's got something to hide which your examination will show up.

One of the first things to check on a Stag is whether or not it is complete. Although the Mark I models came as convertibles or hard tops (and only optionally with both types of top), Mark II models had both hard and soft tops as standard equipment. Hard tops get damaged in storage and even (believe it or not) are sometimes lost by owners who don't use them much, and there are several Stags around without hard tops. New ones are available, but they are pricey. The absence of a hard top on a late car can therefore be a valuable bargaining point when buying.

Bodywork and fittings

Now that even the newest Stags are fifteen years old, corrosion of the bodyshell has become much more of a problem than it ever was when Stag enthusiasm was in its infancy, in the late 1970s and early 1980s. Paradoxically, it is the final, 1976-1977 models which tend to suffer most from superficial rust. In this period, of course, British Leyland was at its lowest ebb, low morale in the workforce led to poor quality manufacture, and — dare we say it — a few corners were probably cut on the production lines in order to save money.

The structure of a Stag means that most of its outer panels are cosmetic. Visible rust in wings and doors does not therefore mean that a major rebuild will be necessary, although it can give a warning of more serious problems underneath. Every one of the outer panels can be replaced or repaired, so some rust need not deter you too much. Be realistic, though, about the amount of work a car will need before it reaches the standard which will satisfy *you*. And if corrosion seems particularly serious, look more closely. You may have come across a car which was quickly patched up after an accident at some time in its history and has now started to rust through from the *inside*. You'll have to use your own judgement on this because a lot of the more serious corrosion is quite hard to detect.

Starting at the front of the car, look for rust in the valance below the front bumper. Then check the panel ahead of the bonnet, in the front wings and around the front wheel arches, where stone damage might have caused sub-surface corrosion. Note the

Above: The chromed 'horseshoes' at both the front and the rear tend to suffer from pitting and dulling, as in this example.

Below: The panel which runs in front of the bonnet can also suffer badly from corrosion, although it isn't always obvious how bad it is unless you strip it right back. The extent of the corrosion on this shotblasted bodyshell is clearly visible.

Rust forms around the front wheel arches like this.

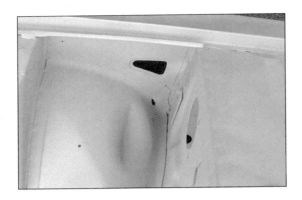

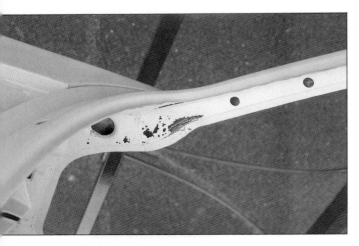

Top, left: Don't forget to look under the bonnet for corrosion damage where the wheelarch meets the inner wing and bulkhead.

Top, right: You'll have to poke around quite carefully to discover corrosion here. These are the box-sections which support the floorpan, just behind the front wheel arch. Damage won't usually be as easily visible as it is on this shotblasted bodyshell.

Above: Visible problems on a windscreen pillar…

Left: … and the not-so-visible kind. Rust here would normally be concealed by the trim.

"From The Cockpit"

The following piece by Mick Walsh appeared in Classic & Sportscar *magazine and is used with their kind permission.*

'I never would have guessed in advance the car that would impress me most this month — a model I'd previously ridiculed for its lack of development, poor reliability and medallion-man image. Yet I find myself considering buying this Anglo-Italian tourer, a design which makes far more sense for Rover to relaunch than a repackaged MGB.

'It's not particularly quick (0-60mph in 10sec and 117mph flat-out), and has a powerhouse that, though torquey, is prone to underbonnet fires and jumping timing claims. Also, an unobservant eye that neglects the temperature gauge could lead to warped cylinder heads. But despite such a reputation, it has one of the largest one-model owners' clubs in the country. The reasons are obvious when you drive a good one.

'With distinctive T-bar framing the sky, and burbling V8 exhaust trailing behind, there's no denying Leyland's seventies flagship has charisma and relaxed charm. If only the new masters of Triumph had executed this inspired idea with German quality, forgotten the siamesed Dolomite engine and ordered up a fresh Buick motor. As a result of lazy engineering only 27,000 were made and yet another great British idea was compromised.

'The car, as you've probably guessed, is the Triumph Stag. Those seventies brochures of the stylish tourer, parked on Monte Carlo's harbour, look seductive today, and the price of a new Nissan Sunny can buy a fine motoring experience — providing the car is properly maintained, of course. If it sported an Italian badge, I'm sure I'd have forgiven its poor reputation sooner. No wonder so many are stolen.'

condition of the chromed 'horseshoes' at the outer edges of the grille-and-headlamp aperture: corrosion here isn't a serious problem but it does give you a bargaining point. If not corroded, they may have lost much of their sheen. The chrome plate on front bumpers can also go dull with time.

Moving now towards the back of the car, check the door skins, which can rust through from the inside, usually near their bottom edges. Open the doors and look at the inner surfaces of the windscreen pillars — a notorious rust-spot on Stags and difficult to repair neatly. Examine the curved section at the base of the door closing pillar, where it meets the outer sill panel. The sills themselves can corrode badly (and beware of cars which have brushed aluminium oversills, as these can hide all sorts of problems). You should look at the inner sills under the car as well, and remember that bad corrosion here is expensive to rectify properly.

Inside the car, lift up the rear seat squab and check whether a leaking convertible top has allowed rust to get a hold. You should pay particular attention to the area around the seat belt mountings in the floor, as corrosion here could prove disastrous in an accident.

Look next at the lower leading edge of the rear wings, where they meet the sills: bad corrosion here can also be expensive to rectify. Rear wheel arches rot out, and the lower edges of the wings behind the wheelarches are often rather dog-eared. The rear bumper and rear 'horseshoe' chrome mouldings suffer in exactly the same way as the fronts, and the valance under the rear bumper can also rust quite badly. Additional problems are rust at the trailing edge of the boot lid, usually just inboard of the chromed edging strip, and damage to the vinyl covering of the hood well cover.

You should also look underneath the car. Re-examine the inner sills and the edges of the floorpan where the two components meet. Look closely at the cross-members under the front seats and the outriggers just behind the front wheel arches. Prod gently at the inner edges of the wheelarches to check for weakness caused by corrosion which has

Left: Even the hard top can suffer. Note the rust on the leading edge of this example.

Below: Rust in the body sills can often be largely concealed by the kick-plates. But don't be lulled into a false sense of security — this is what might be lurking underneath!

Bottom: Water trapped in the bottoms of the doors causes them to rot through like this.

Opposite page: Shot-blasting has revealed the serious corrosion in this shell, where the floorpan has rusted through inboard of the sill and a series of small holes is evident behind the seat mounting. Damage like this would normally be quite hard to detect with seats and carpets in place. Nevertheless, it is potentially lethal: in an accident, the seat could tear away from the floorpan.

not yet become visible. It is also prudent to examine the fuel tank, which can sometimes rust through from the outside.

Lastly, don't forget to look at the hard top, if the car has one (and it should if it is a post-February 1973 example). Rust attacks the leading edge and, if the hard top is left on for long periods, it can spread to the top of the windscreen surround as well. You may well find more rust in the panel which runs below the rear window, especially where it is trimmed with a bright strip.

Interior and convertible top

The standard seat coverings were always vinyl with basket-weave perforated panels flanked by plain panels, and they can split and tear in old age. Leather upholstery was available as a (rare) option, and will crack and discolour if it has not been regularly treated with hide food. If originality matters to you, it will be important to check whether your car has been updated with later seats, or even resurrected with seats from an earlier car. Mark I seats are distinguishable by the plain panel at the top of the front seat backrests; on US-market cars, there were also fixed head restraints at the front. Mark II front seats had perforated vinyl right up to the top of the backrest, and provision for adjustable head restraints. These were optional until 1975, when they were standardised, but in practice a majority of cars seem to have been fitted with them. The upholstery material on Mark II cars was flame-retardant; that on Mark Is was not.

Originality may also be at stake when examining the convertible top of a potential purchase. Not all cars built before February 1973 had one, of course, although all those built after that date did. Pre-February 1973 convertible tops had rear quarter-lights, but the later ones did not. All convertible tops were finished in Mercedes mohair with a beige lining, but the cost of re-covering a hood with this material has led many owners to opt for cheaper materials: double-duck is a favourite.

Air-conditioning was an optional extra until mid-1975, but was very rare. Don't set your heart on finding a car with it fitted.

Top of the Poll

Under the heading TRIUMPH STAG IS YOUR WINNER, the influential monthly Your Classic published the following news item in its April 1992 issue:

'Yet again the Triumph Stag has come top in our readers' poll. You, the readers, have voted it not only the best all-round classic you can buy for £10,000 or less, but also the best looking, and it won by a staggering majority.

'Second in both categories came the Jaguar MkII — another tremendously popular car. In the best all-round section the Stag and Jag were followed by the Morris Minor, Mini Cooper, MGB, Rover P5, Reliant Scimitar, Jaguar XJ6/12, Triumph Vitesse, VW Beetle and Rover P6.

'As for the best lookers, after the two leaders came the Rover P5, Jaguar XJ6/12, Triumph TR6, MGB, Triumph TR4, Alfa Spyder, Jaguar E-Type, Karmann Ghia and Jensen Interceptor.'

(By kind permission of the Editor, Your Classic)

Above: Rust damage to the sill at the rear of the door opening. The kick-plate has been removed for this photograph, to show the extent of the damage.

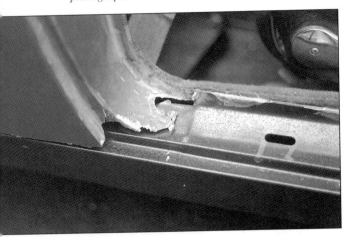

Above: With the sill removed, the full extent of the corrosion damage is evident. This is the other side of the same car.

Opposite page: Advertising for the Stag frequently sought to convey a sophisticated, cosmopolitan image, placing the car in suitably high-profile surroundings and stressing its appeal to the discerning enthusiast. Power, luxury and comfort are all emphasised in this typical example, which comes from a brochure celebrating Triumph's 75th Anniversary.

Engine

This is the Stag's traditional weakness. Proper attention nowadays can make a Stag engine as durable as any other of its age, but only a small proportion of cars receives the care and attention which will ensure this. If the owner of a car you're looking at doesn't produce a sheaf of bills as evidence of the care he has lavished on his Stag's engine, make sure you check very carefully that everything is in order before you buy.

The first thing to check is the state of the cooling system. Does the car run hot? Does the temperature gauge work? (It may have been disconnected to disguise an overheating problem.) Is there anti-freeze or corrosion inhibitor in the radiator? Does the radiator get hot all over? (One which does not may be partially blocked.)

The point of these checks is to look for signs of the Stag engine's biggest problem: overheating. In the early days, quality control at the factory was partly responsible for the problem, as some engines contained swarf and other loose materials which soon blocked up their waterways. Later, the problem was caused by non-inhibited water corroding the water passages in the aluminium cylinder heads, with the result that small pieces of corroded aluminium broke off and were pumped round the system. Inevitably, they caused blockages. (Aluminium corrosion, by the way, can also affect the cylinder head bolts, making them impossible to remove without damage to block and heads.)

Failure to keep the water level up to the required level also caused problems, as the water pump is mounted high up and will obviously not function correctly unless the water level is high enough. The usual result of serious overheating is warped cylinder heads — so watch out for a thick layer of gasket cement around the head-to-block joints, which may be masking the damage temporarily.

The engine's second major problem is wear in the timing chains, which tend to stretch after 25,000 miles or so. This problem will be exacerbated unless regular oil changes have been carried out, not least because poor lubrication can lead to failure of the hydraulic chain tensioners. The chains can then jump sprockets on the timing wheels and allow the valves to hit the pistons.

This is the Grand Touring car that has beaten the continentals at their own game. All over Europe—all over the world—motoring devotees have set their sights (and their hearts) on a Stag. Which is great for Britain. If a trifle frustrating for British Stag hunters. Certainly, this is a car that's well worth waiting for.

Utterly sophisticated in every styling detail, it combines the comfort and luxury of a prestige saloon with the thrust and vivacity of a true sports car. Available as a soft top or hard top plus soft top, it boasts a potent 3 litre, V8 engine, fed by twin Strombergs and capable of launching you from 0 to 50 in a slick seven seconds.

Yet, inside, there is no suggestion of sports car spartanism. Instead, luxury abounds. From you-shaped front seats that recline fully, to electrically operated windows. From thickly-moulded carpeting, to a definitive heating and ventilating system. From aircraft-type, quick-scan instruments, displayed on a non-glare walnut fascia, to a distinctive and generously upholstered roll-over bar.

Stag

No matter what frustrations might occur while buying and restoring a Stag, they all become worth it if the outcome is possession of a car as immaculate as this one. Shown also on the front and back covers of this book, it was restored by the Heathrow Stag Centre.

STAG BUYER'S QUICK CHECKLIST

Even for an experienced buyer, it is easy when inspecting a car to get carried away by one's own enthusiasm or distracted (sometimes deliberately) by the vendor and consequently fail to carry out a properly systematic check. Listed here are all the main points you should take into account when viewing a Stag. If necessary, take this book with you and tick them off one by one. Not only will it save you having to trust your memory, but it will also show the vendor you are not to be duped!

BODYSHELL CORROSION:
- sills
- floorpan
- panels
- hardtop

SOFT TRIM:
- upholstery
- hood covering

ENGINE:
- overheating
- timing chain wear
- oil pressure

AUTOMATIC GEARBOX:
- change quality

MANUAL GEARBOX:
- overdrive operation

REAR AXLE:
- whine

STEERING:
- fluid leaks

SUSPENSION:
- wander

Right: A small fault, but an irritating one: damage to the vinyl surface of the hood well cover, around the catch for the hard top.

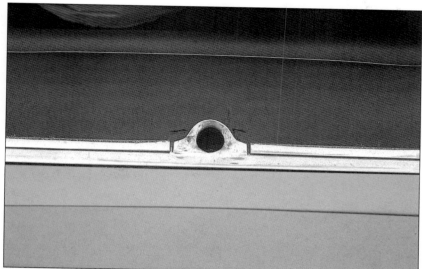

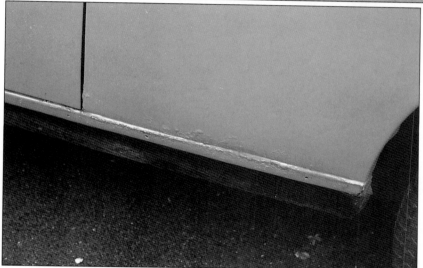

Above: Rust in the rear wing above the sill might not look too bad at first sight...

Right: ... but it could easily be this bad underneath. Again, this is the other side of the same car, where the whole of the bottom of the wing crumbled away when it was being cleaned up prior to sill replacement. The only solution is a new panel or patch-panel.

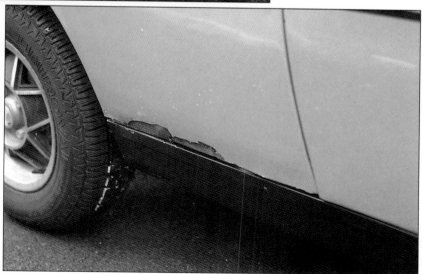

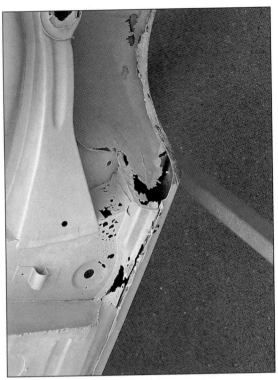

Again, shotblasting reveals what a cursory examination might not: the front inner wheelarch panel is holed just behind the sill.

For that reason, you should always ask the owner of a Stag for sale when the timing chains were last replaced — and ask to see proof in the shape of a bill. You might also ask him what sort of driving he has done in his car, because town driving tends to wear the chains more quickly than motorway work. The best guide to the condition of the chains, however, will actually be your own ears. Listen carefully as the engine is started from cold, and if the chains rattle, they are worn. If so, you'd better start thinking in terms of early replacement, and you'd also better hope that they don't cause a problem before you've got the car home!

The third of the Stag engine's problems is bearing wear. Incorrect machining of the crankshaft journals on early cars caused a number of failures which were dealt with under warranty, but there shouldn't be any untreated early cars around now. However, the dimensions of the crankshaft bearings remained marginal throughout the car's production life. As a result, infrequent oil changes or oil which has thinned out through overheating will cause accelerated wear. Make sure that the oil pressure warning light works and that it does not come on when the engine is idling. Vendors have been known to increase the idling speed of the engine to mask this tell-tale symptom, so check the rev counter to see that the idling speed (with the choke in) settles at 700-750rpm on a manual-transmission car or 800-900rpm on one with automatic transmission.

It should be apparent from all of this that careful maintenance can prevent all the Stag engine's troubles. For that reason, it isn't vital to buy a car which has had a total engine rebuild. If it's been properly looked after — and you can usually get a feel for this sort of thing when you meet the vendor — it could well be as reliable as you could wish for.

Transmission and rear axle

Although manual transmission was standard in theory, some 70% of all Stags were actually delivered with the optional automatic gearbox. A malfunctioning automatic box may be reluctant to change up, it may change roughly, and it may refuse to kick down, but none of these are faults peculiar to the Stag application of the Borg Warner boxes which are, generally, reliable and trouble-free.

On manual gearboxes, second-gear synchromesh was a little weak and will probably give the first indications that an overhaul is needed. Otherwise, manual boxes give no trouble. The gear lever may buzz on a high-mileage car, but this can be rectified by re-bushing and is irritating rather than serious. Overdrive, when fitted (and there were very few cars without it), may be slow to engage or disengage, or may not operate at all. All these faults are relatively simple to rectify and need not be counted as serious.

The differential breather on the rear axle can become blocked, and this can lead to oil leaks and to overheating in extreme cases. Differentials which have suffered in this way and have not been kept topped up with the correct oil may whine. Whining axles are definitely to be avoided when buying a Stag, because the whine usually means the differential is on its last legs. Bargain accordingly!

Right: A line of rust bubbles around the rear wheelarch might mean the car you're looking at has this sort of trouble.

Below: Rear valances suffer badly from rust caused by the accumulation of road debris, which can hold water against the metal. Don't forget to look under the bumper!

Right: Serious corrosion of the waterways in a Stag cylinder head. In this case, the head was scrap: you can also see the marks of the chisel which had to be inserted before the head would come off the cylinder block! This kind of problem is not visible; but overheating is a sure sign that things will end up like this before long.

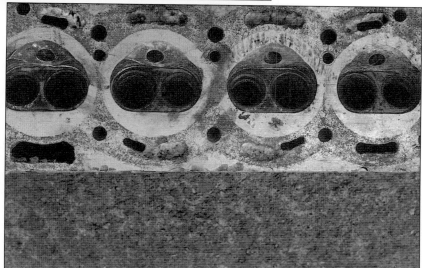

Steering, suspension and brakes

None of these components is particularly troublesome on a Stag. Power steering boxes can leak, of course, and the rubber gaiters on the steering rack should not be split. While neither is a serious fault, both will need to be rectified and both will take time and money. When functioning properly, a Stag's power steering is nicely weighted and does not feel as if it is power-assisted. Over-lightness on the road or over-heaviness at parking speeds will therefore point to problems in this department.

If the car you are inspecting feels sloppy and wanders on the road, the chances are that the rubber bushes in the suspension need to be replaced. Remember that a full suspension re-bush is an expensive job. Suspension ball joints can also wear, but are fairly readily replaced.

Don't worry about what feels like a twitchiness from the rear end under acceleration and deceleration. The symptom is common to all Triumph models with the semi-trailing arm rear suspension, and is caused by the splines of the telescopic drive-shafts jamming (under acceleration) and then freeing (under deceleration). The remedy is simple: lubricate the splines with the constant velocity joint grease specified for Minis.

Brakes generally give no trouble at all, and should pull the car up powerfully and all-square; if not, something is wrong and merits investigation. As far as problems specific to the Stag are concerned, a few road testers claimed that the rear brakes had a tendency to lock early, but this only applies under extreme conditions and can in no way be described as a drawback.

4. Facts and figures

Identifying a Stag

The basic shape of the Stag did not change in its seven years of production, and this makes it relatively easy to update an early car with features from a later example. Whether or not you approve of this practice is for you to decide, but what is important is that some early cars have been passed off as late ones by unscrupulous sellers. In the first instance, the higher prices generally asked for the later cars mean a buyer risks paying over the odds; and secondly, any attempt to restore to 'original' condition is bound to cause frustration and disappointment.

When buying a Stag, therefore, it is important to know exactly what it is you are looking at. The most reliable guides are the **Commission Number** and the **Engine Number.**

Commission Numbers

The Commission Number corresponds to what used to be called the Chassis Number on cars which had a separate chassis and body. It is found on a plate attached to the left-hand-side door shut pillar or (on the last cars) on a plate attached to the top of the left-hand front wing valance. This number should correspond exactly with the one listed in the car's registration document, and you should double-check that it does so.

All Commission Numbers are prefixed with the letters LD (or LE for US-market models). A typical example would therefore be LD 31205. The sequences for Stags were:

LD 1 upwards   1970-1971 models
LD/LE 10001 upwards   1972-season models
LD/LE 20001 upwards   1973-season models
LD 30001 upwards   1974/1975-season models
LD 40001 upwards   1976/1977-season models

Engine Numbers

The Engine Number will be found stamped at the back of the cylinder block, near the distributor. It should correspond exactly with the one in the car's registration document. Engine Numbers are prefixed with the letters LF (or LE for US-market variants), and end with the letters HE (or UE for US-market variants). A typical example would therefore be LF 11246 HE. The sequences were:

LF 1 HE upwards   1970-1971 models
LF 10001 HE upwards   1972-season models
LF 20001 HE upwards   Mark II models

It is of course possible that the engine in a later Stag will have been replaced with a reconditioned unit from an earlier type. This need not cause concern unless originality is important to you.

Other Numbers

Every Stag bears at least three other identifying numbers. A small plate attached to the front crossmember of the body beside the left-hand bonnet hinge gives the **Body Number.** On the gearbox will be found stamped the **Gearbox Number** (automatic gearboxes have this number stamped on a plate), and there is an **Axle Number** stamped on the rear axle casing.

Left: A typical Stag Commission Number plate.

Above: Finding the Engine Number is a little more difficult. You need to look on the engine block in the position indicated by an arrow.

Left: Don't bother with the number on the plates riveted to the body here: it's the Body Number.

Triumph Stag — Technical Specifications

Drive configuration: Front engine, rear-wheel drive.

Engine

Type: 90° V8 with five-bearing, cast-iron block and aluminium alloy cylinder heads with overhead valves. One overhead camshaft per cylinder bank.

Capacity: 2997cc (182.9cu in)

Compression ratio:
LF...HE engines, below 20001: 8.8:1
LF...HE engines, 20001 and above: 9.25:1
LE...UE engines, below 20001: 8.0:1
LE...UE engines, 20001 and above: 7.75:1

Bore and stroke: 86mm x 64.5mm (3.39in x 2.54in)

Maximum power:
LF...HE engines, below 20001:	145bhp DIN @ 5500rpm
LF...HE engines, 20001 and above:	146bhp DIN @ 5700rpm
LE...UE engines, below 20001:	127bhp @ 6000rpm
LE...UE engines, 20001 and above:	127bhp @ 5500rpm

Maximum torque:
LF...HE engines, below 20001:	170 lbs/ft @ 3500rpm
LF...HE engines, 20001 and above:	167 lbs/ft @ 3500rpm
LE...UE engines, below 20001:	142 lbs/ft @ 3200rpm
LE...UE engines, 20001 and above:	148 lbs/ft @ 3500rpm

Fuel system: Engines numbered below 20001: two Zenith-Stromberg 175CD carburettors.
Engines numbered 20001 and above: two Zenith-Stromberg 175CDS (E) V carburettors.

Manual gearbox: Four forward speeds, all-synchromesh, driven through a 9in diameter single dry plate clutch. Laycock A-type overdrive operating on third and top gears optional prior to October 1972. Laycock J-type overdrive operating on third and top gears standard from October 1972 except in certain export markets.
Ratios: 2.995:1, 2.1:1, 1.386:1, 1.0:1; reverse 3.369:1. Overdrive 3rd (pre-October 1972) 1.135:1, overdrive top 0.82:1. Overdrive 3rd (post-October 1972) 1.10:1, overdrive top 0.797:1.

Automatic gearbox:

Pre-October 1976: Borg Warner type 35 with three forward speeds, driven through a torque convertor.
Ratios 2.39:1, 1.45:1, 1.0:1; reverse 2.09:1.

Post-October 1976: Borg Warner type 65 with three forward speeds, driven through a torque convertor.
Ratios as for type 35.

Final drive: 3.7:1

Length: 14ft 5.75in (4420mm)

Width: 5ft 3.5in (1612mm)

Height: 4ft 1.5in (1258mm) with hood erected

Wheelbase: 100 in (2540mm)

Track: Front: 52.5in (1330mm) — Rear: 52.9in (1340mm)

Suspension:

Front: Independent with MacPherson struts, lower links, anti-roll bar and telescopic dampers.

Rear: Independent with semi-trailing arms, coil springs and telescopic dampers.

Steering: Power-assisted rack-and-pinion.

Brakes: Servo-assisted split-circuit system with tandem master-cylinder. 10.6in diameter discs at the front; 9in diameter drums at the rear.

Wheels and tyres:

Pre-October 1975: 5.5J pressed-steel disc wheels with four-stud fixing and push-on trims. Knock-off chromed wire wheels available until mid-1975 only. Five-spoke alloy wheels optional from 1973.
185HR14 tyres (Michelin XAS fitted as standard).

Post-October 1975: 5.5J five-spoke alloy wheels standard. 185HR14 tyres (Michelin XAS fitted as standard).

Weight: 2981 lbs (1355kg) with hard top

The front suspension depended on MacPherson struts.

Production Figures

	Home	Export*	Total
1970	700	40	740
1971	1990	1911	3901
1972	3505	999	4504
1973	4472	974	5446
1974	2606	836	3442
1975	1986	912	2898
1976	2466	644	3110
1977	1372	464	1836
	19097	6780	25877

(*Export figures includes USA)

Notes:

1. These figures are for calendar-year.
2. US sales began in September 1971 and ended in July 1973.
3. The last Stags were built in June 1977.
4. Sales forecasts when the Stag project began were of 12,000 cars per year. By the time of the 1970 UK launch, Triumph still expected to build between 10,000 and 15,000 cars per year.
5. Triumph expected 'conservatively' to sell 2,000 Stags in the USA during the car's first 12 months in that market.
6. Factors affecting sales included the 1973 oil crisis (which mainly affected 1974 figures) and the introduction of facelifted models in February 1973 and October 1975.

Performance Figures

(Manufacturer's figures for manual transmission cars, dated January 1975)

Through the gears:	0 - 30mph	3.5 secs
	0 - 40mph	5.0 secs
	0 - 50mph	7.0 secs
	0 - 60mph	9.0 secs
	0 - 70mph	12.0 secs
	0 - 80mph	15.5 secs
	0 - 90mph	20.5 secs
Top gear acceleration:	30 - 50mph	7.5 secs
	50 - 70mph	8.0 secs
Standing quarter-mile:		17.0 secs
Maximum speed:	120mph	

Notes:

Automatic-transmission cars were slightly slower, typically taking up to 1 second longer for the 0-60mph sprint and having a maximum of about 116mph. US-market cars with emissions-controlled engines were slower still, manual-transmission examples taking an extra half second for the 0-60mph sprint and reaching a 115mph maximum. Examples of contemporary road-tests from the motoring press are available in Brooklands Books' excellent road test series (see Chapter 7).

The independent rear suspension had semi-trailing arms and coil springs.

A view of the 'traditional' Rover V8 transplant, common in the 1970s and early 1980s. This engine is the 155bhp SD1 version. On the standard Rover inlet manifold, the twin SU carburettors were too tall to fit under the Stag's bonnet...

...and so bonnets had to be modified. This neat alteration uses the bonnet bulge from a Ford Capri, grafted on to the standard Stag bonnet. Not all bonnet modifications were this tidy, unfortunately.

One way of getting the Rover V8 under an unmodified Stag bonnet was to use the MG version of the engine, which saw service in the MGB GT V8. However, in unmodified form, this was some 20bhp down on the Rover saloon and Stag engines.

5. Engine transplants

For many years, the reputation of the Stag's engine for unreliability was such that many owners simply did not bother to rebuild an engine which had failed. Instead, they opted to fit their cars with an engine of known reliability. Now that the Stag engine's troubles have been all but developed out by specialists, many of these converted Stags are being re-converted to run original-specification engines. Nevertheless, there are still a good number of cars around which have non-original engines and it is worth looking in some detail at the pros and cons of such vehicles.

The first question is one you have to ask yourself, and it concerns originality. Would you mind having a car which is not to original specification? If the answer is Yes, read no further in this Chapter. If the answer is No, then there are some other significant issues to consider before making a final commitment.

Perhaps the most important question to answer next is whether the conversion was carried out by a reputable specialist or not. Most semi-competent mechanics can bolt a new engine into an engine bay as big as the Stag's, but not every one will fabricate satisfactory engine mountings or ensure that there is enough clearance in all the right places. Some conversions involve bulkhead modifications, and these range in competence from the simple hacksaw job to the neatly refinished.

However, the biggest problem which arises with conversions is that the engines used are often of quite different weights from the Stag's original V8. The implications are manifold. Changing the car's weight distribution is potentially dangerous unless adjustments are made to suspension height, damper rates and brake balance to compensate. Very few conversions have ever taken account of such issues, for the simple reasons that their proper resolution involves extra cost and that the point of installing a non-standard engine in the first place was to *save* money.

Think next about the spares problems you might encounter. Mating a non-standard engine up to a Stag's standard cooling system generally calls for a little ingenuity in finding hoses which will suit. That is all very well if you, five or six years and two or three owners further down the line, know what those hoses came from. But if no-one tells you that your top hose is a cut-down item from a Bedford truck (for example), how are you ever going to find out? Chances are that you will find yourself stranded on a motorway in the middle of the night with a burst top hose and the best that the AA man can offer you will be a tow to the nearest garage.

You should also think pretty carefully about the insurance implications of running a non-standard car. Insurance companies often do not take kindly to modified vehicles (especially where the engine power has been increased), and will load premiums accordingly. Some may also ask for an engineer's report to certify that the conversion has been carried out to an acceptable standard before they will insure a car.

However, Stag engine conversions are not all gloom and doom. Triumph themselves actually looked at revitalising the Stag in the mid-1970s with the Rover 3½-litre V8 engine (in Triumph TR8 form) and five-speed gearbox, and it was

Above: Another well-executed Rover V8 installation, this time using an SD1 engine with an Offenhauser manifold and Holley carburettor. It all fits neatly under the bonnet and offers a hefty performance increase. This car is also fitted with the Rover 5-speed gearbox.

Below: The 2½-litre Triumph engine slots easily into an engine bay which was originally designed around it! The one here is the twin-carburettor version; fuel-injected engines, though more powerful, were notoriously troublesome.

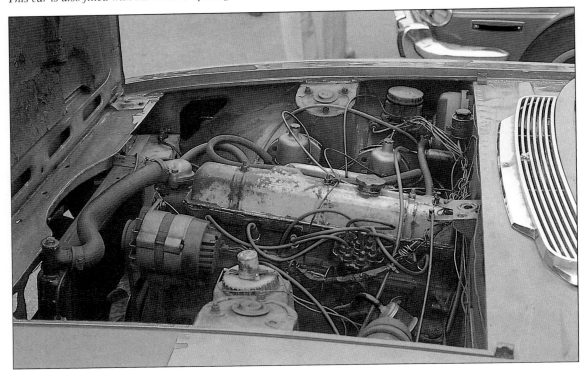

Ford V6 transplants have also been common. The engine fits well into the Stag's engine bay.

probably only British Leyland's decision to stop Stag production altogether which prevented that powertrain from becoming standard. Today, the Rover V8 engine, usually mated to the Stag's own automatic transmission, is one of the better conversions available. The Rover engine gives a little more power in most of its versions, and a lot more in others, and it remains true to the spirit of the original in that it is a V8. However, it is also considerably lighter than the Triumph engine, which causes the nose of the car to sit a inch or so higher on its standard suspension. Suspension and braking changes are therefore vital on a Rover-equipped car. Without them, steering is affected at high speed and emergency braking can be a stressful experience. Most versions of the Rover engine are also too tall to fit under the Stag's bonnet, and bonnet modifications vary considerably in their aesthetic appeal. They are also often irreversible.

Another popular conversion in Stags has been Ford's European V6 engines, either the 3-litre Essex type or (less commonly) the later 2.8-litre Cologne version. As their weight approximates much more closely to that of the original V8 engine, there is no need to make suspension and braking changes. Power is a little down as compared to the Triumph V8, and so performance suffers. And there is no doubt that the V6 exhaust note sounds wrong for a Stag!

Some conversions have used Triumph's own six-cylinder engines, which fit admirably into the engine bay because the earliest Stag prototypes were designed around such engines. However, the 2000 engine leaves the Stag quite badly underpowered, and even the 2½-litre version gives disappointing performance. In theory, the 150bhp fuel-injected 2½-litre as used in the TR5 and early TR6 sports cars should give acceptable performance, but very few people have been prepared to go to the trouble which installing the fuel injection system causes.

In the USA, conversions have drawn on a variety of domestic powerplants. Ford and Buick V6 engines and Ford and Chevrolet small-block V8s have been used; and so, strangely enough, has the Volvo V6. In the USA, however, Stags of any kind are fairly thin on the ground and no company has considered it worthwhile to produce a 'fitting kit' of the type offered by the best of the UK converters. All converted Stags in the USA are therefore likely to be 'work it out as you go along' jobs. You should draw your own conclusions from this!

6. Living with a Stag

If you've already decided that a Stag is the car you want and that no other will do, then nothing anyone can say will make any difference. On the other hand, if a Stag is one of a number of possibilities you are considering, then it will be very much worth your while thinking about what the car would be like to live with. This Chapter is designed to help you think about the issues involved.

The first point to consider is **cost**. Purchase prices fluctuate with fashion and with the state of the economy, so they are not worth considering here. In any case, you presumably already know whether you can afford to buy a Stag in the present state of the market or not. However, what you should be thinking about is the cost of keeping the car on the road and in a condition which *you* will regard as satisfactory.

There is no getting away from the fact that the Stag was designed as a luxury grand tourer for the relatively well-heeled, and that its maintenance costs will always be consistent with that basic design parameter. When new, a Stag cost as much as a high-quality executive saloon, and its running costs will always be consistent with what buyers in that price-bracket were able to afford.

Take its fuel consumption, for example. Manual cars with overdrive are unlikely to better 20mpg; the more common automatics tend to average around 18mpg. Servicing costs will also be high, and it really is important to keep a Stag properly and regularly serviced. Triumph recommended a service every 6,000 miles. Ignore that recommendation at your peril.

If you can look after your Stag yourself, you will undoubtedly save money; but *don't* let a back-street garage look after it, and *don't* try to do it yourself unless you really know what you are doing. Non-experts can make an appalling mess of a Stag in no time at all, and what you'll save in labour charges you'll lose many times over when something fails. The best thing to do is to take your car to one of the acknowledged Stag experts — find out who they are through the owners' club — and have it looked after properly. It won't be cheap, but it will be worth it in the long run.

Insurance will not be cheap, either, although many classic-car insurance specialists will be able to offer attractive rates, usually with the penalty of a limited annual mileage. It is wise to shop around and to get several quotations. Most important, though, will be to get agreed-value cover. This means that the cost of any claim will be considered in the light of the car's true market value. Many owners have discovered too late that standard insurance policies simply rate the Stag as an old car, which to a non-specialist underwriter means it is worth next to nothing. You don't want to be the next one claiming for £1500 worth of accident repairs on a car which your insurers believe is worth only £500.

Storage is also an important consideration. Whether you intend to use the car a lot or not, you will certainly not want to leave it parked in the street overnight. Stags are attractive to joy-riders (and are, sadly, none too difficult to steal), and their popularity as classics makes them attractive to thieves who will either sell them on or strip them for spares. Their well-heeled image also makes

All right then, where are you going to put it when it's not on the car? The Stag's hard top is a bulky item to store, and it takes two people to lift it. If you live alone and have no storage space, you could have a problem...

An oil pressure gauge wasn't standard, but many owners have fitted one as a prudent early-warning indicator of engine trouble. This one has been fitted in an extra pod under the dash...

...and this one has been neatly integrated into the existing dash, where it has replaced the clock.

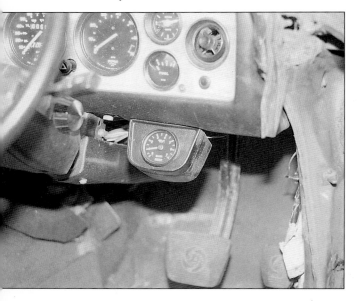

them attractive to the sort of moron who gets his or her kicks by running a key along your car's shiny paintwork.

A Stag will fit into an ordinary domestic garage so, if you've got one, plan to keep the car in it. If not, rent a lock-up. You will probably find that keeping the car in a garage also reduces your insurance premium. In an ideal world, your garage should be a little bit bigger than standard, so that you will have somewhere to store the car's hard top safely when you aren't using it. It takes up more room than you think! Although Triumph never offered a storage stand for the Stag hard top, one is now available through certain specialists and is a worthwhile purchase. In case you were thinking of putting the hard top up in the rafters of your garage in order to keep it safe while you're not using it, we'd suggest you make sure you know just how heavy and unwieldy the top is before you make your final decision!

Storage of the soft top also demands a little thought. Many owners have discovered, to their cost, that the soft top has deteriorated in its well while their car's hard top has been on during the winter months. It is advisable to raise the top once in a while just to make sure that everything is in order and, if the car is going to be stored off the road for a period, it is best to leave the soft top erect.

How **practical** is the Stag as an everyday car? That depends greatly on what you use an everyday car for, of course. If you are single or are only likely to carry one passenger, the seating accommodation will be perfectly adequate. However, rear seat accommodation was really designed for children, and an extra pair of adults in the back of a Stag will complain about lack of legroom, not to mention the minor annoyance of climbing in across the front seats. Even though the Stag is a saloon-sized car, its passenger accomodation is that of a 2+2.

Boot space is generous for this class of car, however. Three adults (or two adults and two children) will find it quite large enough for most of their needs. Luggage for four adults intending to spend more than a weekend away from home, however, could create a problem.

The subject of **modifications** is one which causes heated debate. The question of engine swaps has already been discussed, and whether you want to keep an early car strictly 'original' or are prepared to modify it with parts from a later example is entirely up to you. In either case, though, remember that the unmodified, original-condition car will always be the one which is worth more and easier to sell in years to come.

However, there are some modifications which fall outside these guidelines. These are modifications which have been introduced to deal with the Stag's known weaknesses. One of the more worthwhile is the large-capacity radiator which is available through Stag specialists and gives a reassuring extra margin of safety against the Stag's well-known tendency to overheat. Specialists have also produced stronger cylinder head bolts, and duplex camshaft chains which remove the need for the recommended 25,000-mile chain change. And it is hard to argue with the good sense of an owner who has fitted an auxiliary oil pressure gauge, even if it does spoil the symmetry of the dashboard arrangement.

Lastly, how reliable is a Stag? In spite of all the horror stories you will have heard, a well-maintained Stag is a perfectly reliable car. The emphasis, however, has to be on that maintenance. Only you know how much trouble you're prepared to go to in order to prevent the Stag's well-known problems from affecting your car. Be realistic, or you might be expensively disappointed.

The thriving Stag Owners' Club offers many benefits to its members. It organises events at regional, national and international levels, publishes a highly professional monthly magazine and, among other achievements, is especially proud of the progress it has made in improving the Stag's security. Top picture shows some of the many Stags driven to the European meeting in Akersloot, Holland, in 1987. Pictured below are Club officials from France, Britain, Switzerland, Holland and Germany at the 1990 gathering, held in Llandudno, North Wales.

7. Stag support services

Within the Rover Group, which is today's slimmed-down incarnation of what in the 1970s was British Leyland, the Triumph name has ceased to exist. Rover Group dealers, by and large, simply do not want to know Stag owners. Servicing items are generally available from Unipart outlets, but there is no organised dealer support for Stag owners.

The Stag Owners' Club

Despite the above, the car's popularity has brought about the happy situation that there is a considerable amount of support available through non-franchised specialists. Not the least of the factors in this has been the activities of the well-organised and successful Stag Owners' Club, which in 1991 could boast that, with over 6,000 members, it was the largest single-model enthusiasts' club in the UK.

Membership of the Stag Owners' Club is very worthwhile. The club is run by a National Committee and has over 60 local areas where members can meet to increase their enjoyment of Stag motoring. A problem shared at one of these meetings is, as often as not, a problem solved. Static rallies and other events are held throughout the year at local, national and international levels, and the SOC's annual National Day, held in different parts of the country from year to year, regularly attracts over 700 cars.

All SOC members receive an illustrated magazine of over 60 pages each month. This contains articles on Stag maintenance, local area news, details of forthcoming events, letters from members

and technical queries complete with answers from the Club's consultants. The magazine also carries advertisements for cars and spares.

The Club has good relationships with many of the specialist parts suppliers, and has been instrumental in arranging the remanufacture of unobtainable or hard-to-find items. It also offers special insurance schemes, with a valuation service for members who make use of these schemes.

At the time of writing, the SOC could be contacted through its Membership Secretary, Howard Vesey, 53 Cyprus Road, Faversham, Kent ME13 8HD. (SAE appreciated with your enquiries.) However, Club officials do change from time to time and you would be well advised to check the current contact address in the national classic car magazines.

There is also a small owners' club in the USA. The Stag Club of America can be contacted at P.O.Box 26453, Tucson, Arizona 85276. Again, you should check this contact address in the classic car press.

Stag Specialists

Like Club officials, Stag specialists come and go. However, those listed below are well-established in the field.

Aldridge Trimming, St Marks Road, Chapel Ash, Wolverhampton WV3 0QH, tel. 0902-710805 or 0902-710408. Suppliers of remanufactured interior trim parts. Approved by Heritage, the organisation set up to monitor the activities of those involved in maintaining older cars made by the companies now absorbed into the Rover Group.

S.N.G. Barratt, The Old Workhouse, Union Lane, Trysull, Wolverhampton WV5 7JD, tel. 0902-892307. Heritage-approved Stag spares specialists.

Cardinal Triumph Supplies, Cardinal House, High Level Road, Gateshead, Tyne and Wear NE8 2AG, tel. 091-478-5444. Stockists of Stag spares.

Cox and Buckles, 22-28 Manor Road, Richmond, Surrey TW9 1YB, tel. 081-948-6666. Heritage-approved suppliers of Stag spares.

CPR Engineering, Unit 12, Lowes Lane Industrial Estate, Wellesbourne, Warwick, tel. 0789-470471. CPR can supply most Stag parts from stock, and offer a full restoration service for the cars.

Hart Racing Services, 48 Gorst Road, Park Royal, London NW10, tel. 081-963-0946. HRS is the oldest of the Stag specialists and has been a Heritage-approved company since 1981.

Millstream Motor Company Ltd., Unit 3, Brunel Close, Ebblake Industrial Estate, Verwood, Dorset BH21 6BA, tel. 0202-828101. Servicing and restoration work.

Peak Performance Co. Ltd., (The Heathrow Stag Centre), Peregrine Works, 210/214 Lampton Road, Hounslow, Middlesex TW3 4EL, tel. 081-570-0477 or 081-577-1350. The Heathrow Stag Centre offers a full range of maintenance and restoration services, and also keeps a good selection of Stags for sale.

Regency Classics, 49 New Road, Rainham, Essex, tel. 04027-550572. Regency Classics supply new and used spares, carry out all types of mechanical and restoration work, and keep several Stags in stock for sale.

Rimmer Bros., Triumph House, Sleaford Road, Bracebridge Heath, Lincoln LN4 2NA, tel. 0522-568000. Heritage-approved suppliers of Stag parts.

SOC Spares Ltd., 5 Wheeler Street, Headcorn, Kent TN27 9SH, tel. 0622-891777. Heritage-approved suppliers and remanufacturers of Stag spares. SOC Spares grew out of the Stag Owners Club's own spares organisation and retains close links with the club.

The Stag Centre, 381 Geffrye Street, London E2, tel. 071-739-7052. A long-established company which offers servicing and restoration work, and supplies new Stag parts.

The Stag Workshop, Unit 5, 13 Thrush Road, Parkstone, Poole, Dorset BH12 1LT, tel. 0202-747338/731570 (outside business hours). A personal service to Stag enthusiasts including restoration, servicing, spares, sales.

Surrey Stags, 64B Weyhill, Haslemere, Surrey GU26 1HN, tel. 0428-658427. Sales, servicing, inspection/valuation, restoration, trimming.

TSCS (Triumph Sports Car Specialist), Units 5-8 Bournecrete, Eurolink Trading Estate, Sittingbourne, Kent, tel. 0795-478951. Sales, service and restoration, including cars built to customer specifications.

Tudor Classics, Unit 20, Grecian House, Worsley Road North, Walkden, Greater Manchester M28 5QW, tel. 0204-795341. Full workshop facilities for restoration and servicing. Stag parts suppliers.

E.J. Ward Motor Engineers, 66 Jarvis Street, Leicester, tel. 0533-519775. Specialists in Stags, including restoration, servicing and sales.

In the USA, owners may wish to contact:
The Roadster Factory, P.O. Box 332, Killen Road, Armagh, Pennsylvania 15920, tel. 814-446-4444. The Roadster Factory is a Heritage-approved supplier and is an agent for Cox and Buckles.

Above: The Stag engine does not take kindly to amateur bodging. If yours needs work, you will be better off entrusting it to one of the acknowledged specialists than allowing the apprentices at Joe's Garage round the corner to cut their teeth on it. Of course, if you're an expert yourself…

Below: …there is no shortage of panels to help you rebuild a damaged or rusty Stag. This selection was seen on a trade stand at a Stag Owners' Club event.

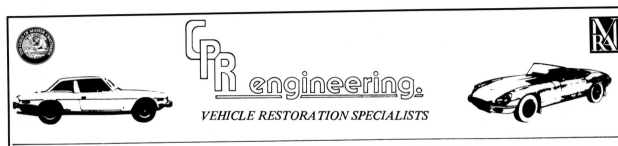

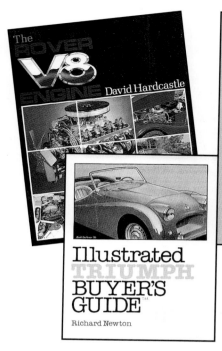

The Stag Library. Practical guides, road test collections and other literature can increase your knowledge and enjoyment of the Stag, even if you think you know it all already!

Stag Books

Everybody likes to take time off from driving a Stag once in a while to sit in a comfortable chair and read about them. Stag devotees, though not as spoilt in this respect as enthusiasts of higher-volume classics, still have a reasonable number of publications to choose from.

Factory literature, in the shape of the full **workshop manual**, the **parts catalogue** and the **owner's handbook**, is available through Brooklands Books (tel. 0932 865051). Brooklands also publish **Triumph Stag 1970-1980**, a collection of road tests and other press articles, while a similar volume, **Triumph Stag Collection No. 1, 1970-1984**, is now out of print but might be found secondhand.

There are valuable lessons to be learned from Kelsey Publishing's **Triumph Stag Restoration**, a reprinted collection of articles which appeared in *Practical Classics and Car Restorer* and includes stage-by-stage coverage by John Williams of a 1972 Mark I restoration.

James Taylor's **Triumph Stag Super Profile**, published by Haynes, provides a concise overview

of the Stag, while for those who value colour plates, over 100 of them are to be found in Andrew Morland's **Triumph Stag** (Osprey Publishing).

Anyone wishing to read about the Stag in its broader context should get hold of Graham Robson and Richard Langworth's **Triumph Cars: The Complete History** (Motor Racing Publications), now in its second edition, which covers both the company and the cars from inception to end of production and is painstakingly researched.

Illustrated Triumph Buyer's Guide, by Richard Newton, is an American book again covering the entire range and with useful advice on each model's relative strengths and weaknesses. Publishers are Motorbooks International.

Owners of Rover V8-engined Stags can read about the history and many uses of that power unit in David Hardcastle's **Rover V8 Engine**, published by Haynes.

Finally, as this book goes to press, James Taylor and Stag Owners' Club historian Dave Jell are preparing a full history of the Stag which will be published by Windrow & Greene.

STAG OWNERS CLUB

ESTABLISHED IN 1979

Membership of the Stag Owners Club now exceeds 6,000. The Club is run by a National Committee and has over 46 local areas where members can meet to increase their enjoyment of Stag motoring.

Local, National and International Meetings are held throughout the year. Our annual National Day attracts over 700 Stags and is held at different locations around the country.

Spare parts are readily available thanks to a host of specialist parts suppliers, many of whom are remanufacturing unobtainable or hard to find items.

There are special insurance terms with a valuation service for members taking part in the schemes.

An illustrated magazine of over 60 pages is sent to all members each month. It features articles on Stag maintenance, local area news, details of forthcoming events, members letters, technical queries complete with answers from the Club's consultants, advertisements and a variety of other information.

A wide range of car badges, T-shirts, key fobs, hats, tankards, magazine binders, etc, are available direct from our Accessories Secretaries.

**For membership details please send a S.A.E. to:
The Membership Secretary, Stag Owners Club,
53 Cyprus Road, Faversham, Kent ME13 8HD**